EAST ANGLIAN TRACTION

John Jackson

First published 2018

Amberley Publishing
The Hill, Stroud
Gloucestershire, GL5 4EP

www.amberley-books.com

Copyright © John Jackson, 2018

The right of John Jackson to be identified as the Author of this work has been asserted in accordance with the Copyrights, Designs and Patents Act 1988.

ISBN 978 1 4456 7294 6 (print)
ISBN 978 1 4456 7295 3 (ebook)

All rights reserved. No part of this book may be reprinted or reproduced or utilised in any form or by any electronic, mechanical or other means, now known or hereafter invented, including photocopying and recording, or in any information storage or retrieval system, without the permission in writing from the Publishers.

British Library Cataloguing in Publication Data.
A catalogue record for this book is available from the British Library.

Origination by Amberley Publishing.
Printed in the UK.

Introduction

The East Anglia area has long fascinated me, chiefly because it is an area of many contrasts. It boasts the hustle and bustle you would expect from its towns and cities. Then, at the opposite end of the spectrum, the quiet tranquillity of its countryside reflects an unhurried way of life. This way of life has seemingly remained unchanged for generations. So, what do East Anglia's railways offer in twenty-first century Britain?

For a start, there has been much debate as to the definition of 'East Anglia'. For the purposes of this book I have confined it, loosely, to the counties of Norfolk, Suffolk and Cambridgeshire. Further to the west of this area sits the Cambridgeshire city of Peterborough. This city is an important railway gateway to the area. Its rail activity is only touched on here as the variety of traffic justifies a book all to itself.

Taking a look at East Anglia's rail map, it's obvious that one line dominates. The Great Eastern Main Line (GEML) from Norwich to London's Liverpool Street runs broadly north to south through the region, with Ipswich as an important junction on its route through Suffolk and on to Essex and the capital.

The half-hourly passenger services on this 'core' London route remain in the control of GA's fifteen Class 90 locomotives. This makes East Anglia one of the last bastions for UK loco-hauled passenger trains. Additionally, some London-bound stopping services starting at Ipswich (and at Norwich in the case of a few peak-time services or loco substitutions) are handled by electric multiple units (EMUs).

Several lines survive around the coast serving towns such as Great Yarmouth, Lowestoft and Sheringham. Both Ipswich and Norwich are also served by lines that run inland to destinations such as Cambridge and Peterborough. This means that towns such as Thetford, Newmarket and Bury St Edmunds still feature on today's passenger railway map.

Felixstowe retains a passenger service to and from Ipswich, which operates alongside the procession of freight trains that share this route in order to reach the UK's busiest container port. This uneasy alliance between rail companies is all the more remarkable given that the Felixstowe branch is, for the most part, a single-track railway.

The Suffolk town of Sudbury is perhaps more fortunate. It retains a link to the rest of the rail network via a 12-mile branch, branded 'The Gainsborough Line', which runs south to Marks Tey and connects there to the Great Eastern Main Line. The Stour Valley line beyond Sudbury towards Cambridge was just one of the region's casualties under the infamous Beeching Axe of the 1960s.

These secondary lines are chiefly served by diesel multiple units (DMUs). Norwich's Crown Point traction maintenance depot is responsible for the servicing of the area's fleet of twenty-six DMUs, consisting of five Class 153s, nine Class 156s and twelve Class 170s. The fifteen Class 90s, together with their driving vehicle trailers and the sets of hauled coaching stock, are also maintained here. The 'home' fleet is often augmented by hiring in an additional Class 90 from DB Cargo. The depot also houses two Class 08 shunters to handle the stock movements around the depot complex.

Further, an ongoing shortage of serviceable Class 153 and 156 units has resulted in some services from Norwich to Great Yarmouth and Lowestoft seeing regular usage of 'short sets' of coaching stock. These are hauled by the popular Class 37s and 68s provided by a hire-in arrangement with Direct Rail Services.

The majority of passenger services in the area have been operated by Greater Anglia since 2016 as the 'East Anglia' franchise. This is a joint business venture between Abellio (the Dutch rail operator) and Japanese company Mitsui. One of the operator's chief pledges was the replacement of over 1,000 carriages during the 2020s, thereby eliminating virtually all existing stock, including the fleet of Class 90 locos. In this publication, we take a look at the traction used on passenger services in the run up to these promised replacements.

In the west of the region, services operate between London's Liverpool Street and King's Cross stations to Cambridge, Ely and King's Lynn. These 'Fen Line' services are handled out of King's Cross by Govia Thameslink Railway and by Greater Anglia out of Liverpool Street. The Great Northern services are in the hands of a fleet of Class 365 and Class 387 EMUs while Greater Anglia uses some of its Class 379 'Stansted Airport' units on services north of that airport towards King's Lynn.

Both companies serve the new station at Cambridge North, located in the suburb of Chesterton, which opened for business in May 2017. My first impression on visiting was that there was a new era as transport interchanges go: the car park holds 450 cars but the cycle park has space for 1,000 bicycles.

Finally, to the extreme west of East Anglia sits the city of Peterborough. Today's station (previously known as Peterborough North) sits at an important railway crossroads. Lying some 75 miles north of London, it is served by a good percentage of the Virgin Trains East Coast (VTEC) intercity services linking King's Cross via the ECML to cities in the north of England as well as Scotland. It is also the northern terminus of Great Northern's stopping service from the capital using Class 365 and 387 EMUs.

VTEC's fleet of thirty-one Class 91 electric locos is complemented by a similar number of Class 43 High Speed Trains, or HSTs, which not only operate on the non-electrified lines but also regularly 'under the wires' to destinations such as Leeds and Newcastle. These services are scheduled to be handled by Virgin's next generation of units from 2018 onwards. A fleet of sixty-five Class 800/801s is under construction. In the meantime, cover for this VTEC fleet is provided by the regular hire-in of additional HST power cars from East Midlands Trains' depot at Neville Hill, Leeds.

Peterborough also benefits from its retention of rail services from east to west across England, particularly when many comparable towns and cities lost theirs in the 1960s. Firstly, Cross Country Trains operate an hourly service from Birmingham New Street through Peterborough to Cambridge and Stansted Airport. Secondly, East Midlands Trains also offer an hourly service that connects Liverpool and Manchester to Norwich, running via Sheffield and Nottingham. The Cross Country Trains services are operated by Class 170s and the East Midlands Trains (EMT) services by Class 158s with occasional Class 156s. EMT also provide a service to the Lincolnshire towns of Sleaford, Spalding and Lincoln using single-car Class 153s. Finally, Greater Anglia provides a two-hourly service from Peterborough to Ipswich provided by Class 170, and occasionally Class 156, units from Crown Point depot.

The area's freight traffic is centred on the UK's busiest container port, Felixstowe. The port is served by a non-electrified branch from Ipswich. This is the main reason Freightliner has a major loco stabling point there, handling both diesel and electric locomotives. The movement of freight trains in the Ipswich area was helped considerably in 2014. In March that year a new mile-long chord was opened, allowing traffic to and from Felixstowe to reach the West Coast Main Line (WCML) via Peterborough and Nuneaton without the need for train reversal in Ipswich yard. Some workings, however, do still reach their destination by routing via the Great Eastern Main Line and the London suburbs.

This important container traffic is augmented by a handful of other freight services in the region. Many of these are infrastructure trains in connection with ongoing maintenance and improvement work by Network Rail. Worthy of mention is the infrastructure yard at Whitemoor, near March, to the west of the region. Built on part of the site of the former March marshalling yard and diesel depot, it incorporates the National Track Materials Recycling Centre. The Whitemoor complex sees regular traffic from places as diverse as Doncaster to the north and Hoo Junction, near Higham in Kent, to the south. East Anglia also sees aggregate traffic movements for the wider construction industry. A few other examples are also featured on these pages.

Once a year, the small yard at the Suffolk town of Stowmarket springs into life. It becomes the hub for the region's Rail Head Treatment Trains. These are despatched from here to counter the rail industry's annual battle with the autumn leaf fall.

East Anglia is a region of railway contrasts and the mix of passenger workings, together with some examples of the remaining freight traffic, is demonstrated in this book.

It is an area that I have known and loved since childhood. This book features a wide variety of locations across the region – from the platforms of its bigger city stations, to some of the most rural locations still served by Britain's railways.

I hope you enjoy your browse!

John Jackson

East Anglia's flagship passenger service sees Norwich and Ipswich linked to London's Liverpool Street station by a half-hourly service. These trains are routinely in the hands of Greater Anglia's (GA) dedicated fleet of fifteen Class 90 electric locomotives. On 24 September 2015, No. 90007 *Sir John Betjeman* is seen at the buffer stops at London Liverpool Street, waiting to propel its train to Norwich. These locos complete the 115-mile journey in around two hours.

At the northern end of the service, No. 90015 *Colchester Castle* waits at Norwich on 29 September 2016. It will haul its train to London's Liverpool Street with a driving vehicle trailer (DVT) on the rear. The locos are placed at the London end of services, with the DVT at the Norwich, or 'country', end of the trains.

At the opposite end of the traction spectrum can be found a small fleet of GA's one, two or three-car diesel multiple units. These can be found across the region's non-electrified lines. A typical East Anglian scene on 4 May 2014 sees a single-car unit, No. 153309, calling at Hoveton & Wroxham while working a Sheringham to Norwich local service.

To the west of the area covered by this book, No. 170205 is seen at Cambridge on 23 May 2017. The three-car unit is waiting to commence its journey to Norwich, just under 70 miles away. These services cover that distance in approximately an hour and a half.

The regional passenger services around Norfolk are generally in the hands of Greater Anglia's fleet of diesel multiple units (DMUs). Their lack of availability has, however, regularly seen substitution by hired-in locomotives and coaches in order to maintain these services. On 8 July 2015, No. 37425 *Concrete Bob/Sir Robert McAlpine* waits at Great Yarmouth to return its train to Norwich.

These locos and coaches are hired in from Direct Rail Services (DRS). Two locomotives are required to top'n'tail these coaches and No. 37405 is seen at the opposite end of the stock at the buffer stops at Great Yarmouth. The popularity of these loco-hauled 'short sets' among rail enthusiasts is evidenced here. As a result, these services also enjoy swelled passenger numbers and resultant revenue.

On the arrival of the Pendolinos on Virgin's West Coast, the driving vehicle trailers (DVTs) were released. Some of these DVTs were moved to the Anglia Region to work in partnership with their Class 90 locomotives. On 8 July 2015, DVT No. 82143 is seen at Ipswich. At a quick glance, it could be described as a 'loco lookalike'.

It is customary for these DVTs to be at the Norwich or 'country' end of the rake of coaches. Here, DVT No. 82103 arrives at Norwich to complete its journey. The Class 90 is working at the rear or 'London' end.

Volumes of freight traffic in East Anglia have, like almost everywhere else in the UK, seen considerable decline over the years. Today, the rail movement of containers to and from the Suffolk port of Felixstowe accounts for a sizeable percentage of the remaining traffic. On 2 May 2014, No. 66724 *Drax Power Station* is about to enter Ipswich tunnel with a working from Felixstowe to Hams Hall, near Birmingham.

The various freight operators have a choice of routes to and from Felixstowe. GBRf-owned No. 66724 was heading eastwards to reach the London suburbs before heading north on the West Coast Main Line towards Birmingham. By contrast, Freightliner's No. 66420 is travelling across country to reach its destination. On 30 August 2017, it is seen approaching Manea in Cambridgeshire on a working from Leeds to Felixstowe. Note the semaphore signalling still in use here.

Ipswich is served by the half-hourly Norwich to Liverpool Street services in the hands of Class 90 locomotives. Additionally, an hourly semi-fast service operates from the Suffolk town to the capital. These services are in the hands of electric multiple units (EMUs). On 23 May 2017, four-car No. 360118 waits at Ipswich to commence its journey.

These services are also worked by four-car Class 321 units, strengthened in the peak periods. On 29 September 2016, No. 321423 waits at the rear of a twelve-car service to Liverpool Street. These peak time trains occupy the full length of platform 4 here at Ipswich station.

Services from London towards Cambridge and King's Lynn in the west of the region are also operated exclusively by EMUs. King's Lynn is served by an hourly service operated by Great Northern. On 12 October 2016, No. 365503 is being serviced prior to returning to the capital's King's Cross station.

These Great Northern services are complemented by additional peak-time trains operated by their competitor, Abellio Greater Anglia (AGA). These services do not operate at weekends. On 4 May 2014, a Sunday, No. 317656 was therefore stabled out of use at King's Lynn, awaiting Monday morning commuters.

Cross Country Trains operate a broadly hourly service into the western fringe of the region. Their trains link Peterborough, March, Ely and Cambridge by way of a Birmingham New Street to Stansted Airport service. On a wet 30 August 2017, three-car No. 170102 pauses at March, working that day's 14.34 service towards Stansted Airport.

The town of Waterbeach is one of several that see these Cross Country Trains services passing without stopping. On 1 September 2017, No. 170101 is seen passing through the station.

East Midlands Trains operate an hourly service from Norwich to Liverpool's Lime Street station. Their two-car Class 158 units are the mainstay of these services (with trains strengthened further into their journey, between Nottingham and Liverpool). No. 158812 waits at Norwich on 23 May 2017. It will take around five and a half hours to reach Liverpool.

Another Class 158 unit waits at Norwich on 5 October 2015. At the time, this unit, numbered 158889, was on hire to East Midlands Trains from its sister operator, South West Trains.

In addition to its staple diet of EMUs to and from London, King's Lynn sees the occasional visit of a Pullman service from London Victoria. On 12 October 2016, No. 67012 waits while the empty stock is serviced.

These workings require the stock to be top'n'tailed and, on this occasion, No. 67012 was partnered with No. 67006 *Royal Sovereign*. It will lead the stock when it leaves King's Lynn later in the day.

Two of Norwich's fleet of DMUs are required to operate the services from Norwich to Cromer and Sheringham. These operate to an (almost) hourly timetable. On 4 May 2014, single-carriage No. 153309 is seen passing East Runton, between Cromer and Sheringham, heading back to Norwich.

Norwich to Cromer and Sheringham is predominantly a single-track railway. Additionally, trains are required to reverse at Cromer in order to traverse the section beyond towards Sheringham. The second unit operating services on 4 May 2014 was a two-car unit, No. 156417, and it is seen here in Cromer platform, awaiting departure after the train crew had swapped ends.

A pair of DRS Class 68 locos are often pressed into service on the Yarmouth and Lowestoft branches from Norwich. No. 68003 *Astute* is seen in the station sidings at Norwich between duties on 23 May 2017.

These pairs of locos, like the Class 37s, operate in top'n'tail mode. On 23 May 2017, No. 68022 *Resolution* was at the opposite end of the sidelined rake of coaches.

Freightliner has a share of the movement of aggregates to the East Anglia area. On 20 July 2017, No. 66604 is shunting its wagons at Trowse, just south of Norwich, having recently arrived from Tunstead, near Buxton in Derbyshire.

On 1 September 2017, a Friday, it's the turn of No. 66615 to work into East Anglia from Tunstead. This time its delivery was to Kennett, near Newmarket. The loco is seen pausing briefly at Ely on its return journey. The rake of wagons will be stabled at Barrow Hill, near Chesterfield, for the weekend.

The four-car Class 379 Electrostars were ordered primarily for the Stansted Express services out of Liverpool Street, usually working in pairs. They are also regular visitors to Cambridge. On 8 July 2015, No. 379012 is seen at Cambridge.

On the same day, No. 379004 is seen running adjacent to Cambridge's platform 1. At a little over 500 yards in length, this is among the longest platforms in the UK. I well remember walking the length of it as a very young lad. It seemed to go on for ever!

In 2016, Greater Anglia dropped the 'Abellio' from its title and with it commenced a rebranding of its stock. On 23 May 2017, unit No. 170208 is seen at Stowmarket in its new guise. It is running a few minutes late on a Cambridge to Ipswich service. This particular unit, No. 170208, had previously sported a unique branding to promote 'The Breckland Line' from Norwich to Cambridge, as seen elsewhere in this book.

The former livery can be seen here on another three-car unit, No. 170207. The unit is pictured at Ipswich on 29 September 2016.

The current fleet of fifteen Class 90 locos dedicated to GA's passenger services replaced the ageing Class 86s around the turn of the century. The turn-round scheduling often means two trains occupying adjacent platforms at Norwich. On 20 July 2017, Nos 90010 and 90005 are captured between duties. No. 68005 is in the background.

These Class 90s have enjoyed a variety of liveries over the years. A side view of No. 90008 on 5 October 2015 reveals its Abellio Greater Anglia branding. It is glimpsed from the window of a Class 37-hauled 'short set'.

DB Cargo also handle traffic to and from the port of Felixstowe. On 20 July 2017, No. 66198 heads south through Stowmarket on a working from Wakefield.

The recently opened Bacon Factory chord at Ipswich Europa Junction allows traffic such as this to reach the port without using either Ipswich station or yards. No. 66198 is seen using the new facility just twenty minutes after the picture above.

The first numbered Class 90, No. 90001 *Crown Point*, is seen passing Bethnal Green station in East London on 24 September 2015. It is approaching journey's end on an early evening arrival at London's Liverpool Street from Norwich.

The loco proudly sports the nameplate *Crown Point*. GA named the loco in 2014 in recognition of that depot's contribution to the running of services in the area since the early 1980s. This is its nameplate on 24 July that year, not long after the name had been unveiled.

Norwich's Crown Point depot uses two Class 08 shunters to facilitate stock movements around its complex. On 20 July 2017, No. 08847 is seen in the company of Nos 90009 and 90013, together with examples of its fleet of passenger coaching stock.

On 8 July 2015, No. 90005 *Vice-Admiral Lord Nelson* is stabled alongside the Crown Point facility, awaiting its next turn of duty.

Ipswich is one of Freightliner's most important hubs. With its proximity to the port of Felixstowe, it sees a regular flow of locos to and from the port. They also make use of the adjacent yards and train crew depot here. On 2 May 2014, No. 66591 is seen waiting for action at the stabling point.

On 20 July 2017, No. 66528 *Madge Elliot MBE Borders Railway Opening 2015* has just passed through the station and into Ipswich Yard. It is at the head of a late running Bristol to Felixstowe liner. The photo is taken from a passing Class 170 unit.

Great Northern services between King's Cross and Ely are now divided between Class 365 and Class 387 EMUs. On 1 September 2017, Nos 387120 and 387103 are seen passing Waterbeach.

A minute later, an eight-car formation consisting of Nos 365536 and 365517 is seen heading through Waterbeach in the opposite direction.

GA has a small fleet of five Class 153 units. These single-carriage trains feature on rural services out of both Ipswich and Norwich. On 29 September 2016, Nos 153309 and 153314 are both to be found at the buffer stops in Norwich station between duties.

A year earlier, on 5 October 2015, No. 153335 is to be found at Norwich in more or less the same position, awaiting its next working.

Freight traffic travelling cross-country to reach Felixstowe must negotiate the single-track bottleneck between Ely and Soham. Barway half-barrier level crossing is approximately half way between these two points. First, No. 66709 *Sorrento* approaches the crossing, heading towards Ely with a container train from Felixstowe to Birch Coppice, near Tamworth.

Just a few minutes later, Freightliner duo Nos 66567 and 66534 *OOCL Express* are on the approach to Soham, heading in the opposite direction with a Leeds to Felixstowe liner.

The Class 90s have sported many liveries while working in East Anglia. This was the order of the day in 2013. No. 90013 *The Evening Star* arrives at Ipswich on a working to London Liverpool Street. At the time of writing, the loco has been de-named.

No. 90009 was chosen to recognise the Queens's Diamond Jubilee in 2012. It was named *Diamond Jubilee* that year and was suitably adorned with the Union Jack. On 28 June 2013, it is passing Bethnal Green while working from Norwich to Liverpool Street.

The popularity of the Class 37s, with their 'short sets' of coaches, sees little sign of waning. On 16 June 2016, No. 37422 is seen arriving at Norwich on the rear of a working from Great Yarmouth. It would, therefore, be at the head of the train on the next trip to the coast.

Its partner that day was No. 37419 *Carl Haviland 1954–2012*. This loco is seen a little later in the day, awaiting departure from Great Yarmouth, leading on the return working to Norwich.

Several stations in the remoter parts of the region enjoy a very limited passenger service. Lakenheath, for example, has no scheduled service whatsoever on weekdays and only a handful of services stop on request at weekends. On 2 May 2015, East Midlands Trains' No. 158863 passes through the station.

The service from nearby Shippea Hill is even worse. It boasts only one calling service each day, in one direction only, on request. Not surprisingly, it is among the least used stations on the national rail network. This time, it's the turn of No. 158865 to be seen passing through.

The New Measurement Train is a regular Network Rail visitor to Cambridge, bringing two of the three yellow-liveried High Speed Train power cars to the city. On 5 October 2015, No. 43013 was the power car at one end.

Its partner that day was No. 43062 *John Armitt*. The pair regularly complete circuits of the area before returning to their Derby base.

In 2014, GB Railfreight took over the running of the sand trains from Middleton Towers to King's Lynn. These trains are operated for Sibelco UK from its base near Middleton Towers station, which was closed in the 1960s. On 12 October 2016, No. 66762 waits to come off the branch at King's Lynn on a working to Goole.

On 30 August 2017, No. 66742 *ABP Port of Immingham Centenary 1912–2012* is seen passing through Whittlesea with another working from Middleton Towers. This time the train is destined for Monk Bretton, near Barnsley, in South Yorkshire.

East Anglian Traction

35

DRS locos outbased at Norwich are often called upon to haul a variety of stock moves in the area. On 29 September 2016, No. 68004 *Rapid* was itself working light engine from Crewe to Norwich when called upon to pick up a DVT in London. It is seen passing through Ipswich station.

The DVT on this occasion was No. 82112. It had received attention at Bounds Green and was being returned to its home at Norwich Crown Point.

Norwich's DMU fleet is in such short supply that multiple workings are uncommon. On 12 October 2016, this three-car combination is seen approaching Ely with single-carriage No. 153306 leading.

Its two-car partner on this occasion was No. 156416. The pair are again captured waiting in the platform at Ely station.

A spare DRS loco is often to be found within the area of Norwich station. On 20 July 2017, it's the turn of No. 68002 *Intrepid* to be stabled.

Two months earlier, on 23 May 2017, the spare loco was a Class 37. No. 37605 is seen here partially hidden by the station wall.

March has a long history as an important railway junction in the west of the region. It boasted a seven-platform station a century ago. Today its use is confined to just two platforms. On 30 August 2017, East Midlands Trains unit No. 158863 passes platform 2 on its journey towards Ely and Norwich.

March is served by GA with a two-hour frequency service between Ipswich and Peterborough. On 30 August 2017, two-car unit No. 170271 calls at platform 1 on its way to Peterborough.

Ipswich is an important interchange between local and intercity services. The London and Norwich-bound services call within a minute or two of each other, aiding connections and timetabling. On 8 July 2015, No. 90004 *City of Chelmsford* is seen arriving on a London-bound service.

On the same day, across on the northbound platform, No. 90012 *Royal Anglian Regiment* is just leaving, bound for Norwich.

The East Anglia area sees a number of aggregate workings to and from the quarry at Mountsorrel in Leicestershire. On 1 September 2017, No. 66121 approaches Chettisham level crossing, near Ely, with an unidentified eastbound loaded working from this quarry.

A couple of days earlier, on 30 August 2017, and under threatening skies, No. 66118 approaches Whittlesea. This loaded working is from Mountsorrel to Barham, just north of Ipswich.

Lowestoft has also enjoyed its fair share of locomotive-hauled passenger services in 2017. On 20 July, No. 68005 *Defiant* sits at the buffer stops having arrived with the 12.05 departure from Norwich.

Sister loco No. 68024 *Centaur* was at the rear on arrival at Lowestoft. This loco is captured here waiting to lead from Lowestoft back to Norwich. The turn-round time here is such that the pair will depart less than ten minutes after their arrival.

Potter Logistics in Ely has a long association with the rail industry. On 10 July 2013, their complex was home to two Class 08 shunters, both sporting yellow colours. Nos 08202 and 08598 are viewed from a passing unit.

More recently, on 20 July 2017, No. 47815 was visible in their complex when passing. These Rail Operations Group locos are regularly used to haul various items of rolling stock to Potter's for storage. Indeed, several miles of additional track has been installed by the Potter Group specifically for this purpose.

Three Horse Shoes, near Turves in Cambridgeshire, is the setting for these two passenger workings. Cross Country Trains three-car No. 170637 approaches one of several level crossings on this back road from Whittlesey into March. It is heading to Birmingham New Street on a service from Stansted Airport.

A few minutes earlier, new-liveried GA two-car unit No. 170208 passes Three Horse Shoes on an Ipswich to Peterborough service. The signal box here once controlled the junction for a freight-only branch to Benwick. The line was, however, closed in the 1960s and the track lifted. The signal box survives.

A new station was opened at Cambridge North on 21 May 2017. It is located in the suburb of Chesterton and close to Cambridge Science Park. Its features include a park for up to a thousand bicycles. Two days after it opened, GA four-car unit No. 317513 waits to work the 11.15 service to London Liverpool Street.

Great Northern also serve the new station at Cambridge North. Here, an eight-car formation, with No. 387128 leading, calls on an Ely to London King's Cross working.

East Anglia's association with DRS locos on branch line passenger work goes back a number of years. For example, 10 July 2013 saw the Yarmouth services in the hands of its Class 47 locomotives. No. 47813 is seen at the buffer stops at Norwich that day.

Its partner was No. 47818, also pictured here at Norwich. It is ready to haul the short set of coaching stock back to the coastal town of Great Yarmouth.

GA's fleet of Class 170 units are gradually receiving their new liveries. On 20 July 2017, three-car unit No. 170202 is still in its previous livery. It is seen here at Cambridge about to work that day's 10.10 service to Norwich.

Another example, No. 170206, is seen later that day at Stowmarket. This unit was working an Ipswich to Cambridge service.

Two-car Class 156 units are the mainstay of GA services between Ipswich and Lowestoft. On 29 September 2016, No. 156412 waits at Ipswich to form a service to Lowestoft.

At the coastal end of the line, No. 156418 waits at Lowestoft on 20 July 2017 to head in the opposite direction with the 13.07 departure to Ipswich. With almost simultaneous arrival of units from both Norwich and Ipswich, Lowestoft offers a convenient point to 'swap' units to return them for maintenance, etc. Not so, of course, if Class 68s are substituted, as can be seen here.

Ely station is one of the busiest in the region, with services running to a variety of destinations operated by East Anglia's four passenger operators. On 1 September 2017, East Midlands Trains two-car unit No. 158866 is seen arriving from Liverpool Lime Street. The unit will reverse in the station and continue its journey to Norwich.

Ely is also served by trains on the 'Fen Line' between Cambridge and King's Lynn. On 3 May 2015, Great Northern unit No. 365519 has just passed over the level crossing while working from London King's Cross to King's Lynn. The unit carries a promotional livery advocating Peterborough as the Environmental Capital.

Cross Country Trains serve Ely by way of the hourly service between Birmingham New Street and Stansted Airport. On 1 September 2017, No. 170102 is seen arriving from the Midlands, heading for the airport.

The fourth operator serving Ely is Greater Anglia. Their two-car unit, No. 170271, is seen waiting here on 20 July 2017 on a service from Ipswich to Peterborough.

Stowmarket enjoys what is broadly an hourly service to London with roughly half of the Class 90-hauled services between Norwich and Liverpool Street calling at the town. On 20 July 2017, No. 90010 passes through without stopping on its way to London. This loco had previously carried the name *275 Railway Squadron (Volunteers)*.

Just a couple of minutes earlier, No. 90002 *Eastern Daily Press* had called at the station and is seen propelling the 14.55 service to Norwich northwards.

Little variety of freight traffic is on offer within East Anglia. One flow that has survived, albeit with a much-reduced frequency, is the movement of North Sea gas condensate between North Walsham and Harwich. On 8 July 2015, No. 66704 *Colchester Power Box* heads through the centre road at Ipswich on the loaded working to Harwich.

These GBRf-operated services run once or twice a week at present for Petrochem Carless. On 20 July 2017, it was the turn of No. 66747 to work this service. It is seen approaching Stowmarket with the loaded southbound working.

Part of GA's 2017 pledge within its new franchise has been a commitment to replace all its rolling stock. Meanwhile, its Class 317 units, which date from the 1980s, soldier on. They are seen on services linking Cambridge with the capital. Here, No. 317660 is stabled in one of Cambridge's south bay platforms between duties on 16 June 2016.

The Class 317 duties are chiefly confined to peak hour services. On 29 September 2016, a pair of units, Nos 317657 and 317659, are seen at 10.00 hours waiting to work north on to the local stabling point until later in the day.

Felixstowe proudly claims to be Britain's biggest and busiest container port. Freightliner is one of the biggest players in the movement of these containers by rail. On 29 September 2016, No. 66550 is seen at East Suffolk Junction, Ipswich (from a passing Class 90-hauled service). It has just left the branch from Felixstowe and is about to head westward towards the London suburbs and the West Coast Main Line. Its destination is Lawley Street in Birmingham.

A couple of hours later that day, another Freightliner loco, No. 66420, is seen facing the opposite direction with a container train bound for the port. This loco is one of several Class 66s acquired from Direct Rail Services and it has only just been repainted into its new owner's colours.

The range of stock handled by Greater Anglia's Norwich Crown Point Depot can be seen in this view on 20 July 2017. Two-car unit No. 170273 and loco No. 90013 are kept company by several GA coaches.

In recent years, it seems that Crown Point has had to cope with more than its fair share of unit casualties. For example, No. 170204 was involved in a collision in April 2016. It is seen, complete with tarpaulin, outside Crown Point on 16 June that year.

DRS-owned Class 37s are regulars around the region. They are contrasted by the occasional visit by other members of the same class. For example, Colas-liveried No. 37116 was stabled at Cambridge on 20 July 2017. It was at one end of a Network Rail Test Train (in the company of No. 37057, not shown).

On 12 October 2016, Rail Operations Group-operated No. 37884 was another visitor to the area. It is seen approaching Ely, having dragged unit No. 442424 from Eastleigh to be stored at the nearby Potter Group sidings.

The village station at Manea, on the Ely to Peterborough line, is one of those that has survived into the twenty-first century. It is served by both Greater Anglia and Cross Country Trains and, indeed, passenger numbers appear to be on the increase. East Midlands Trains do not, however, call there, and No. 158812 passes through the station and over its level crossing on 30 August 2017 while working from Liverpool to Norwich.

A few Cross Country Trains services do call at Manea, but not this one. No. 170519 passes, also on 30 August 2017, with a Birmingham New Street to Stansted Airport service. In common with many places in the region, semaphore signals are still in use on this stretch of line.

The routine of half-hourly GA Class 90-hauled passenger trains is broken occasionally. At Ipswich on 8 July 2015, No. 90002 *Eastern Daily Press* takes the centre road as it heads south through the station on an empty stock movement towards London.

Of greater interest to the enthusiasts are the occasions when it becomes necessary to hire in Class 90s to cover for non-availability of their own class members. On 16 June 2016, DB Cargo's No. 90034 provides the power as it propels a Norwich-bound service away from Ipswich.

The line south of Cambridge sees little regular freight traffic. On 8 July 2015, GBRf-owned No. 66706 *Nene Valley* waits at Cambridge while working a Foxton to Willesden Euro Terminal service. These trains operated in order to move spoil from the major Crossrail construction project.

Foxton itself enjoys a regular service into London King's Cross. On 9 September 2017, No. 387122 is seen passing the level crossing and signal box, having just called on a Cambridge North to King's Cross service. The branch to Barrington veers off to the right.

The branch line from Ipswich to Felixstowe has retained its passenger service, which is usually provided by a single-car Class 153 unit. On 8 September 2017, the unit involved is No. 153306, seen here at Felixstowe waiting to form the 10.28 to Ipswich. The unit shares the branch with the intensive freight service to and from the Felixstowe port terminals.

Another branch line survivor in East Anglia is the one from Marks Tey to the Suffolk town of Sudbury (with its Gainsborough Line branding). On 8 September 2017, No. 156418 waits to leave Sudbury with 12.26 to Marks Tey. The line is promoted as 'The Gainsborough Line' – promotional branding being carried by unit No. 156412. There is no freight conflict on this branch and the unit has the branch to itself. Sudbury, however, is isolated from other Suffolk rail destinations without customers making a lengthy detour via Marks Tey, Colchester and Ipswich.

The Norfolk town of Thetford enjoys regular passenger services provided by both Greater Anglia and East Midlands Trains operating between Ely and Norwich. On 7 September 2017, No. 158865 calls on a service towards Norwich.

Around ten minutes later, it's the turn of Greater Anglia unit No. 170201 to call, heading in the same direction but with additional stops. The unit is seen approaching the station, passing the now closed Thetford signal box.

Class 68 substitution on the Norwich to Lowestoft services was due to end on 8 September 2017. The day before, No. 68028 leads the short set away from Reedham working the 14.24 to Lowestoft.

No. 68001 *Evolution* is the locomotive on the rear. It will, of course, lead on the return leg from Lowestoft. The alternative route to Norwich, via the isolated station of Berney Arms, heads off to the left with the Lowestoft route veering right.

A single platform at Newmarket continues to offer a passenger service between Ipswich and Cambridge. Two and three-car Class 170 units are the norm. On 9 September 2017, No. 170204 arrives on a Saturday morning service to Ipswich. About a dozen passengers were waiting to board.

The line remains single-track until it joins the main line to Ely just to the north of Cambridge station. On the same Saturday morning, two-car unit No. 170273 has just entered the single-track section eastbound and is seen near Six Mile Bottom while working the 11.44 Cambridge to Ipswich.

The eastern end of Ipswich station sees a number of Freightliner light engine manoeuvres taking locos between the stabling point and the yards on the opposite side of the main line. On 20 July 2017, No. 66560 is seen making such a move, requiring two reversals to reach the stabling point.

On 2 May 2014, the signalman had not one but two moves to contend with. No. 66416 is making a similar move towards the stabling point while electric loco No. 90049 waits for the signal to back on to a liner, which will head west under the wires towards the London suburbs and thence to the West Coast Main Line.

Single-track sections are scattered across the East Anglia area. The Lowestoft to Ipswich line has lengthy stretches of single line. To the north of the route, units are timed to pass using the loop at Beccles' platforms. First to arrive on 7 September 2017 is No. 170270. It arrives from Lowestoft and will leave on the 15.25 service to Ipswich.

The Class 170 awaits the arrival of No. 156417, which has occupied the single-line section between Beccles and Halesworth. Excellent punctuality means both trains can leave on time. The Class 156 unit will head east on the 15.25 to Lowestoft.

DRS Class 57 locos also visit the East Anglia region. They can be found working the Rail Head Treatment Trains during the leaf fall season. During the rest of the year, they are something of an 'odd job' loco. For example, on 10 October 2015, No. 57008 has arrived at Norwich with an empty stock move involving two GA coaches.

Despite the reduction in operational examples, Freightliner Class 70s also pass through the region on container traffic to and from Felixstowe. On 30 August 2017, No. 70015 is seen passing March East Junction signal box with a working from Felixstowe to Crewe. This particular service is routed via Peterborough rather than the London suburbs.

The scene at Barway, between Soham and Ely, typifies the railway through the Fens. As well as demonstrating the flatness of the surrounding countryside, note the complete lack of lineside fencing in these two shots. No. 170270 is seen heading east on a Peterborough to Ipswich service on 1 September 2017.

Once No. 170270 has cleared the single-track section, No. 170271 is free to pass in the opposite direction about a quarter of an hour later with the reverse working from Ipswich to Peterborough.

The village station at Whittlesford was re-designated as a Parkway station in 2007. It enjoys regular GA services to and from Cambridge and London Liverpool Street. On 9 September 2017, No. 379012 heads an eight-car formation on a service bound for the capital.

Whittlesford Parkway is also served by an hourly service linking Cambridge with Stansted Airport. These services are usually operated by GA's older Class 317 units. On the same day, No. 317514 arrives from Stansted working the 12.26 service to Cambridge.

The station at Trimley, on the Felixstowe branch, witnesses the passing of all freight services to and from Felixstowe regardless of whether they are using the North or South Terminal. On 8 September 2017, No. 66526 is seen passing through the station with a Felixstowe North Terminal to Crewe liner. No. 66507 waits in the background.

No. 66507 has run light engine from Felixstowe's South Terminal. Once its stablemate (No. 66526 above) has cleared the section, the loco can reverse at the end of Trimley station and run light engine to the North Terminal. The railway to Felixstowe is actually two separate single-track lines beyond this station. No. 66507 is seen here heading in the direction of North Terminal after this reversal.

Whitemoor was a major marshalling yard at March, in Cambridgeshire, which had a particularly important role during the Second World War. Today it is home to a Rail Recycling Centre. It receives trains from various parts of the country, including Hoo Junction, near Higham in Kent. This service is operated by Colas Rail and usually brings either a Class 66 or Class 70 to the region. On 30 August 2017, No. 66850 arrives on the inbound working.

It will reach the yard by way of a spur to the right of the Peterborough line. The Colas loco is seen here taking the single-line spur – and into the undergrowth! A similar spur is used by traffic bound for Whitemoor arriving from the Peterborough direction.

The Cambridgeshire villages of Shepreth and Meldreth are served by Great Northern services between Cambridge and London King's Cross. An hourly calling pattern is maintained throughout the day. On 9 September 2017, No. 365502 calls at Shepreth on the 13.14 service to Cambridge North.

On the same day at nearby Meldreth, No. 387118 leads an eight-car formation passing non-stop on a service from King's Lynn to King's Cross.

One of the busiest sections of line in East Anglia takes in the stations of Stowmarket and Needham Market. At nearby Haughley Junction, north of Stowmarket, the line to Ely branches off from the Great Eastern Main Line between London and Norwich. On 8 September 2017, No. 90006 passes the long-closed station at Haughley on the rear of a Norwich-bound service.

A few minutes earlier, No. 66765 had just traversed the junction at Haughley. It is seen leaving the line from Ely and heading south towards Stowmarket. It will reach Felixstowe using the recently installed curve at Europa Junction, Ipswich. This container train originated at Masborough (Rotherham, South Yorkshire).

The town of Whittlesey (the station retains the spelling 'Whittlesea'), between Peterborough and March, sees a limited stopping service from both East Midlands Trains (EMT) and Cross Country Trains. On 30 August 2017, EMT's No. 158858 is about to pass through the station working a Norwich to Liverpool Lime Street service.

Half an hour later and No. 170397 is also seen passing through the town without stopping. Here, it passes the same point near Whittlesey, working a Stansted Airport to Birmingham New Street service.

The use of Direct Rail Services' Class 68s may have come to an end in East Anglia, at least for the time being. The popular Class 37s, however, continue on branch line duties, attracting the attention of enthusiasts across the country. On 23 May 2017, No. 37419 arrives at Norwich on the 13.17 service from Great Yarmouth.

On this occasion, it is stablemate No. 37405 that is seen bringing up the rear. This loco was delivered new back in 1965 and so has clocked up fifty years' service. It carried the name *Strathclyde Region* for a number of years.

It is business as usual at Norwich on 29 September 2016. No. 90003 waits at the London end of the 13.00 service to London Liverpool Street. The loco was not carrying its name, *Raedwald of East Anglia*, on this date.

There was disappointment on 23 May 2017, however, as the stock arrived to form 14.00 service to London. It was a unit substitution in the form of No. 321349 (leading No. 321360) that arrived on the inbound working from Liverpool Street, causing a few enthusiasts looking forward to Class 90 haulage to delay their journeys by half an hour.

The port of Felixstowe is responsible for a growing percentage of the freight traffic carried across the East Anglian region. At the time of writing, there are sixty-six workings a day to and from the port – thirty-three in each direction. Two of GBRf's workings on 30 August 2017 are featured here. First, No. 66766 approaches March station with a working bound for Masborough (Rotherham).

About ninety minutes later, sister loco No. 66756 *The Royal Corps of Signals* is again heading west. This time the location is Manea and the train's destination is Doncaster.

GBRf is an important player in the movement of containers by rail from Felixstowe. It is Freightliner, however, that operates around three quarters of all the services to and from that port. On the afternoon of 8 September 2017, two liners pass Needham Market within half an hour of each other. First, No. 66597 *Viridor* heads north on a service to Doncaster.

Heading in the opposite direction, No. 66957 *Stephenson Locomotive Society 1909–2009* passes south through the station on a working from Leeds to Felixstowe.

Since the late 1990s, the thirty miles of line from Norwich to Cromer and Sheringham has been branded 'The Bittern Line'. The bird of the same name can be found in the line's environs. On 4 May 2014, No. 156417 is seen arriving at one of the intermediate stations, Hoveton & Wroxham.

The unit, No. 156417, has since been adorned with a branding initiative encouraging people to 'Ride the Bittern Line'.

Class 158 units are routinely allocated to East Midlands Trains' services between Liverpool and Norwich. As already mentioned, units are usually paired on the Liverpool to Nottingham leg with one of the pair going forward to Norwich. On 12 October 2016, No. 158788 arrives at Ely, where trains reverse.

On occasion, Class 158s are unavailable and Class 156 units are substituted east of Nottingham. One such unit, No. 156411, is seen here waiting time at Ely on 27 April 2014.

The lines from Ipswich to Lowestoft and Felixstowe have been jointly branded as 'The East Suffolk Lines' – and unit No. 156407 carries a related promotional branding. On 7 September 2017, sister unit No. 156417 is seen at Westerfield, where these two branch lines split.

Class 170 units are also to be found on East Suffolk Lines services. On 7 September 2017, two-car unit No. 170271 arrives at Saxmundham working the 16.40 to Lowestoft. A branch line from here to Sizewell still sees occasional nuclear flask traffic operated by Direct Rail Services to and from its base at Sellafield in Cumbria.

The lines from Norwich to Great Yarmouth and Lowestoft are branded as 'The Wherry Lines'. The name derives from the river boat to be found on the Norfolk Broads. Indeed, unit No. 156409 carries a related promotional branding. Some services have enjoyed loco-hauled workings over the last few years. On 23 May 2017, however, two-car unit No. 156416 waits at Norwich to form the 13.16 service to Great Yarmouth.

Another Class 156, unit No. 156422, arrives at Lowestoft on 30 September 2014 on a service from Ipswich. Despite the tight turn-round, this unit will be swapped here and work the 13.48 service to Norwich. The impressive array of semaphore signals here are scheduled to be replaced by Network Rail. The contract to carry out this work was recently awarded with target completion by spring 2019.

On 20 July 2017, two freight trains were simultaneously looped at Ely at around 17.00. First, No. 66755 is seen against the backdrop of Ely Cathedral as it waits for the unit from Ipswich to clear the single-track section. The photo was taken from that unit, No. 170271, as it approaches Ely.

DB Cargo was also represented by No. 66015. It is seen waiting in the goods loop to follow No. 170271 towards Peterborough. It is working the returning empties from Ely to Peak Forest in Derbyshire.

The small communities of Thurston and Elmswell, to the east of Bury St Edmunds, have retained their passenger services through the hourly service between Ipswich and Cambridge. On 8 September 2017, three-car unit No. 170204 calls at Thurston, working the 13.49 service from there to Cambridge.

On the same day, and an hour or so later, No. 66063 heads through Elmswell with DB Cargo's Wakefield to Felixstowe service. This is one of several the operator runs daily to the Suffolk port.

The rural charm of East Anglia's railways can be summed up in these two views. On 2 May 2015, No. 170203 passes through Shippea Hill on a Cambridge to Norwich working.

On a quiet Saturday morning, sister three-car unit No. 170204 disturbs the tranquillity as it passes through Kennett on a Cambridge to Ipswich service. The date is 9 September 2017.

Needham Market witnesses the passing of Greater Anglia's flagship service between London and Norwich but without calling. On 8 September 2017, Driving Vehicle Trailer No. 82133 leads a Norwich-bound service through the station. Taking freight and passenger train movements into consideration, ten moves an hour are the reward for watching trains passing through the station here.

On this occasion, its partner, providing the power, was No. 90012 on the rear. This loco carries the name *Royal Anglian Regiment*.

Crown Point Depot in Norwich is responsible for the maintenance and availability demands placed on its Class 153 and 156 units, among others. Here, on 16 June 2016, No. 153314 is glimpsed on the depot's number 13 road from the window of a passing Class 37-hauled working to Great Yarmouth.

At the opposite end of the depot, a two-car Class 156 unit, No. 156416, is stabled on 29 September 2016. This time the shot is taken from the window of a Class 90 bound for Ipswich and London.

The intermediate stations on the Ipswich to Felixstowe branch offer the chance to see all freight workings to and from the port. On 7 September 2017, GBRf loco No. 66770 heads through Westerfield, working a Felixstowe to Hams Hall (Coleshill, Warwickshire) service.

The next day, sister loco No. 66744 *Crossrail* heads past Bury St Edmunds Yard signal box while working another container train from Felixstowe. This time its destination is Doncaster. It is about to pass No. 66616 in Bury yard. The Freightliner loco had arrived earlier on a stone working from Tunstead, north of Buxton in Derbyshire's Peak District.

Two more container trains destined for Felixstowe are seen in these views as they head across country through the region. On 1 September 2017, No. 66014 is seen near Barway, between Soham and Ely, while working from Wakefield to the Suffolk port.

A couple of days earlier, on 30 August 2017, No. 66598 approaches Whittlesea station with a working from Lawley Street Freightliner Terminal in Birmingham to Felixstowe.

There's nothing like a pair of 'Tractors' to disturb the afternoon silence in deepest Norfolk. On 7 September 2017, No. 37716 leads the 13.17 from Great Yarmouth to Norwich as it pauses, in vain, in the hope of custom at Brundall Gardens station.

That day, No. 37405 is the partner loco. It is seen here on the rear as the working leaves on the final leg of its journey. Their next stop is Norwich, just three miles away.

It is approaching thirty years since the Class 321 electric multiple units were delivered new bearing the distinctive Network South East livery. They are still regular performers on the semi-fast services from Ipswich to London. On 10 July 2013, No. 321329 sits in platform 4 at Ipswich as it waits to head back to London at the rear of a twelve-car formation.

The opposite end of the same platform is seen here on 20 July 2017. This time unit No. 321326 is at the front of the formation, waiting to work the 15.52 service to London Liverpool Street.

The Freightliner stabling point at Ipswich still receives its fuel by rail. The tanks are worked to Ipswich from Lindsey on Humberside. On 5 October 2015, No. 66556 is seen shunting a short rake of fuel tanks at the stabling point.

On 23 May 2017, there are three Class 66 Freightliner locos visible on the stabling point alongside a rake of fuel tanks. At around 15.00, Nos 66516, 66532 and 66559 are seen between duties.

Until its recent repaint, three-car Class 170 unit No. 170208 sported a promotional livery. This unit is seen at Ely on 12 October 2016 with all three coaches promoting 'The Brecks'. The Brecks is an area of West Norfolk that is popular with visitors, measuring nearly 400 square miles and including Thetford Forest.

Ely is one of my favourite locations, partly because you just never know what might turn up at the station. While taking the above photo, Freightliner's No. 66585 *The Drax Flyer* passed in the opposite direction, working light engine from Washwood Heath (Birmingham) to Parkeston (Harwich).

Sometimes a locomotive's livery soldiers on from a bygone era. That's certainly true of Freightliner's Class 90 electric locomotive No. 90048, seen here on 30 September 2014. It carries two-tone grey bands, complete with a red triangle. This is in part a hangover from its Trainload days within British Rail. It is seen here on Ipswich's stabling point awaiting its next duty. At the time of writing, the loco still carries this livery.

A very different livery is to be found at Norwich on 30 September 2014. Direct Rail Services' No. 68013 is seen bearing Chiltern Railways' silver colours. This is in recognition of the two companies working together on loco-hauled services out of London Marylebone. On the above date, however, its role was that of DRS spare loco at the Norfolk city.

Peterborough is the gateway to East Anglia for thousands of passengers as well as many freight services to and from the region. For this reason, it's deserving of a book of its own. Its inclusion here is therefore limited to a brief look at the operators serving the city. There is a two-hourly service operated by Greater Anglia (GA) between here and Ipswich. On 26 January 2017, No. 156407 waits at Peterborough to leave on the 15.50 service to Ipswich.

GA Class 170s are more common on these services. On 9 October 2014, two-car unit No. 170273 waits to leave on the 13.50 service to Ipswich. It will follow the East Midlands Trains-operated service to Norwich, worked by No. 158780, from the adjacent platform.

Virgin Trains East Coast services are also about to be transformed. On 23 March 2017, their services were in the hands of its fleet of Class 91 electric locos, working side by side with pairs of HST power cars. Here, No. 43309 (once named *Leeds International Festival*) is on the rear of a service overtaking No. 91120 (formerly named *Royal Armouries*), which is just leaving the platform on its way to London King's Cross.

Great Northern operate semi-fast services between Peterborough and the capital, using a mixture of Class 365s and Class 387s, often in pairs. On 30 June 2017, No. 387111 is waiting to leave the city, forming the 15.19 service to King's Cross.

The services operated by both Hull Trains and Grand Central pass through the station without a mandate to stop there. On 28 January 2016, Hull Trains-operated No. 180110 passes through Peterborough while heading south on a service from Hull to King's Cross.

Grand Central also uses Class 180 units on many of its services. On 30 June 2017, No. 180107 is seen heading north through Peterborough station on a King's Cross to Bradford Interchange working.

East Midlands Trains also operate a local service between Peterborough, Spalding and Doncaster (via Lincoln). These services are usually in the hands of their single-car Class 153 diesel multiple units. On 14 June 2017, No. 153379 arrives on a service from Lincoln. It will then form the 11.50 service to Doncaster.

The West Coast Railway Company operates regular charter services to and from East Anglia. These usually involve its ageing fleet of Class 47 and Class 57 locomotives. On 23 March 2017, No. 47746 *Chris Fudge 29.7.70 – 22.6.10* is seen reversing in the station platform. It had arrived from Southall in West London via the East Coast Main Line. It will then head east to Norwich for use in conjunction with one such charter.